Tongues: The Elevation of a Mystery

Bert Farias

Published by Holy Fire Ministries-Bert Farias, 2023.

Table of Contents

WHAT FRIENDS/READERS ARE SAYING ABOUT THIS BOOK:

Reading, *Tongues: The Elevation Of A Mystery,* was incredible. It was a holy impartation! Even if you are flowing in the gifts regularly, I believe this book will take you deeper into those gifts. My prayer language actually changed as I gave a corporate tongue, and the depth of the interpretation increased with its authority. This is just one instance of how Bert Farias' book affected me, and I am sure it will do at least this for you. In my opinion, this is Bert's best book. Thank you for sharing this revelation with us. — **Joe Crain**

UTTERLY CONTAGIOUS! I dare everyone who calls themselves "Spirit-filled" to read this book without speaking in tongues—it won't happen! You will want to stop several times and focus on speaking and singing in tongues as it wells up within you! I was born into all things Charismatic, being fully-entrenched and "dyed in the wool." Like the author, I have had growing concerns about the lack of demonstration of the Baptism of the Holy Spirit in our churches and the paucity of invitations to receive this glorious gift. By my mid-twenties, my tongues-rich childhood had mostly vanished in "Spirit-filled" churches, being relegated to some back room or small group experience, at best, so as to not run off newcomers. Spirit-filled in name only... Tragic! It ought to never be.

The Body of Christ sorely needs discipleship on tongues and their purpose, and Brother Bert has taken up the mandate. Tongues are the rivers of living water flowing out of our beings that create life and healing wherever they flow! May our tongues be loosed, in Jesus' Name, with the fresh fire of God that Brother Bert speaks of in these pages! This book is a great place to start. Sending up three cheers for a sequel! What a precious gift Jesus has given His people, and what a dynamic book to give us more insight into it! As an added bonus, it's broken down for every reader; a short read with high-density yields, easy to absorb even for the busiest of lives. — **Lily McBride**

Very informative, completely scriptural, and extremely relevant and important for the times in which we are living. Bert's book has encouraged me to speak in tongues much more than I already do. New realms of the Kingdom are opening up to me from spending quality time each day praying in tongues. Very encouraging and empowering! — **David W. Gillespie**

I had the privilege of reading this powerful new book. It is a revelatory read, being very biblical and doctrinally sound on a controversial subject! Bert has written this profound book in such a way that anyone who reads it can understand it. You will be blessed by his illustrations and challenged to pray in the Spirit more in your walk with Jesus.

In a time where the Deceiver, Satan, has made the personal use of tongues controversial, the Spirit of God has used Bert to bring clarity and understanding regarding the power of praying in other tongues — the means by which we build up ourselves on our most holy faith! — **Christopher Keller**

I found, *Tongues: The Elevation Of A Mystery,* to be a very good resource to help "kick it up to another level" as we seek to re-educate the current Body of Christ about Tongues. As Jesus said in Matthew 13:52 (KJV), "'*Therefore every scribe which is instructed unto the kingdom of heaven is like unto a man that is an householder, which bringeth forth out of his treasure things new and old.*'" I have found some new nuggets of truth to add to my arsenal, as well as reminders of the importance of praying in tongues. — **Dr. Kirk A. DuBois**

I am Spirit-baptized and have used tongues for 47 years, but I gotta say that I learned some new "stuff" reading Bert Farias' work on tongues. Well done, Bert. Well done indeed! — **Carman Ruggeri**

As with all the books Bert has written, this book is challenging, inspiring, and EXACTLY what the church needs IN THIS HOUR! He has a gift of explaining spiritual concepts and helping the reader know how to apply the principles in practical ways. This book is for all believers — those who have not yet received the baptism with the Holy Spirit with the evidence of speaking in tongues; those who have received tongues but don't practice them regularly; as well as those who pray in their Heavenly language daily. It will instruct and provoke all readers to the "*more*" that is readily available for us all. This book is a must-read. — **Christina Hugie**

This book is fresh and with new realms of revelation. Even some things I've already learned from some of the old-timers were jumping off of the page! It's like Mary, sitting at the feet of Jesus, choosing and gleaning the good things that cannot be taken from her! I cannot put this book down! I am receiving impartations from previous revelations! I am catching what has been taught. I am a Holy Ghost "tongue talker" and not ashamed of the Gospel of our Lord Jesus Christ! The devil dare not even try, even if he could, to take this supernatural endowment from the body of Christ! Saints, pray, pray, pray, in the Spirit and magnify God with your most holy faith! I'm only on chapter 3! You can see that I am stirred up, fired up, and not putting up, and don't intend to quit! Like the old-timer once said, "I want men and women to come and watch the Church burn for Jesus!!! Hallelujah!!!" —**Lady Pearlene Tindle**

As a product of the Charismatic renewal of the 1970's, I was blessed to see the outpouring of the Holy Spirit across many churches and denominations, here in Australia. The things which characterized it more than anything were the gifts of the Holy Spirit, including healings, prophetic utterances, tongues, and interpretations. People were alive with the love of God and yearning for evermore of an intimacy with Him. As some denominations or churches became more respectable, the outward signs—particularly tongues—began to wane. In some, the lamps began to dim and their first love started to dissipate.

Brother Bert Farias' book, *Tongues: The Elevation Of A Mystery*, is a timely reminder of the necessity of this wonderful gift. In this clearly-written and highly-readable book, he explains the difference between the personal gift of tongues, to be used in our prayer language every day, and the gift of tongues as should be used in the church setting. He refutes the teachings against tongues, explaining how it has never ceased from the time of Pentecost until today. Throughout this well-written book, one hears the call of God, through the pen of Brother Bert: *Return to Pentecost!* — **Pastor Alan Jones, Australia; Founder, Kingdom Mission International**

Bert Farias writes enthusiastically about this subject that he is so passionate about. And how right he is to do so! This extraordinary gift of prayer, to a great extent, is ignored and even abandoned within Christendom at-large. It seems to me that the strategy of the enemy to distract and discourage individuals and the community of believers from praying in tongues has largely succeeded. Like the proverbial lobster in the boiling pot, the voice of the believer has, over time, become quieter and quieter to the point of muteness. Bert Farias has, for years, recognized this and seeks to blow a trumpet to awaken the body of Christ from her slumber and to embrace the privilege and power of praying in the Spirit. I would dare to suggest that the general failure to pray in the Spirit is directly related to the lack of potency within the body of Christ. Oh, if we only have ears to hear! Blow that trumpet, Bert! Blow! — **Mark Baylis, United Kingdom**

I just finished reading, *Tongues: The Elevation Of A Mystery*, and I'm in awe of all the information I received from it! Wow, there's so much I didn't know about the subject!! A total revelation to me about the importance of consecration and holiness required in praying for myself and others...that is, if I want effective prayers, I must first consecrate myself to God and live holy as He is holy. The importance of that cannot be overstated. I'm still digesting all the teaching within the book and praying the scriptures as well. I thoroughly enjoyed it and learned so much I didn't know!! I recommend this book to all believers. — **Michelle Wolfe**

OTHER END-TIME ORACLES BY THE AUTHOR

1.   *Soulish Leadership*
2.   *Purity Of Heart*
3.   *The Journal Of A Journey To His Holiness*
4.   *The Real Spirit Of Revival*
5.   *The Real Salvation*
6.   *The Real Gospel*
7.   *The Real Jesus*
8.   *My Son, My Son (A book to raise hero children)*
9.   *Prayer: The Language Of The Spirit*
10. *Passing On The Move Of God To The Next Generation*
11. *Cleansing The Temple: Restoring The Glory Of The Lord*
12. *The Tumultuous 2020s And Beyond*
13. *The Supernatural Church Of Love And Power*
14. *The Coming Restoration*
15. *The Nature Of The Kingdom of God*
16. *Divine Order And The Glory Of The Local Church*
17. *Shaping Local Churches For The Move Of The Holy Spirit*

* To read a synopsis of any of these books and/ or to place an order, please visit our website, **holy-fire.org**.

* If this book or any of the author's books are a blessing to you, kindly post a review.

* Thank you for supporting the works of unknown writers who

publish the word of the Lord.

FOREWORD

The New Testament Church was born on Pentecost and launched from the Upper Room under the glorious leadership of the Holy Spirit. It was the continuation of the ministry of Jesus Christ, with His signs and wonders streaming from them as they went. Luke begins his 2nd book, The Acts of the Apostles, with this context-setting statement:

"In my first book I told you, Theophilus, about everything Jesus BEGAN to do and teach" (Acts 1:1 NLT).

The Book of Acts is not the story of a change of command with a hand-off, but a CONTINUATION. Jesus had already set the tone and method of His ministry and it was perfect. Shortly after the launch at Pentecost, Peter stands before the Gentile centurion, Cornelius, and his household, testifying to the Lordship of Jesus. Here's the account from Acts 10:38, 44-45 (ESV).

...how God anointed Jesus of Nazareth with the Holy Spirit and with power. He went about doing good and healing all who were oppressed by the devil, for God was with Him....While Peter was still saying these things, the Holy Spirit fell on all who heard the word. And the believers from among the circumcised who had come with Peter were amazed, because the gift of the Holy Spirit was poured out even on the Gentiles. For they were hearing them speaking in tongues and extolling God. Then Peter declared, "Can anyone withhold water for baptizing these people, who have received the Holy Spirit just as we have?"

Peter summarizes the pattern of Jesus' ministry as the result of being filled with the Holy Spirit—God being with Him as evidenced by doing good and healing all who were oppressed by the devil. There is no way that this pattern of all that Jesus BEGAN to do, could be CONTINUED with any less power than the Holy Spirit's infilling. Jesus had given strict orders that no ministry was to be initiated until they were filled and under the Spirit's power. Peter knew, when he heard Cornelius and the gathered assembly all speaking in tongues and glorifying

God, that he had just witnessed the same baptism with the Holy Spirit that they had received in the Upper Room.

The divine pattern is clear. Speaking in tongues, in its various applications and purposes, is at the heart of the Spirit-filled New Testament Church. And this manifestation, with its edifying purposes, spreads with the Gospel through all the early churches. So germane to the Gospel mission of the Church, is the manifestation of tongues, that its use is codified with extensive testimony and instruction by Paul in his letter to the Corinthian churches.

In 1 Corinthians 14:5 and 18, Paul declares that he speaks in tongues more than any of them and wishes they would do the same. Tongues is not a practice that the New Testament church should (or even *could*) ignore and do without and still operate at the level of its calling as outlined in the Book of Acts.

Recent decades have witnessed a precipitous decline of tongues, leaving a giant spiritual vacuum in the Church and, by extension, in society. And Satan has rushed in to fill the void with deception and evil, resembling the antediluvian world and the days of Sodom and Gomorrah. As a result, today we are experiencing the contradictory elements of the rise of Big Box Churches (think Walmart and Home Depot) juxtaposed against a numeric decline of Christianity. Christianity is rapidly declining in American culture, while the culture of "church" is increasing without advancing the Kingdom. What are we missing?

Bert Farias has written a wonderful book, *TONGUES: THE ELEVATION OF A MYSTERY*, detailing the purpose, methods and applications of this awesome manifestation of the Holy Spirit's working, supported with scriptural explanations and testimonials. This book ought to be given to every Christian who is serious about fulfilling Jesus' assignment to the Church and the world. At some point, as you read through the chapters, the realization will dawn on you that most of the Church's praying has been floundering in the paralyzing grip of mental stagnation. We've been trying to build effective prayers with uninspired minds. We do not know what to pray for as we ought (Romans 8:26b ESV), or how to phrase our praying, but the Holy Spirit is in us to help. Bert does a great job of explaining how the use of tongues brings our minds under the influence of the Holy Spirit, providing God's direction for prayer and service.

The Church was never intended to succeed in its mission without this essential operation of the Spirit. Bert lays out the important distinction of private and public, devotional and prophetic applications of tongues, with detailed explanations. Tongues has been wrongly classified as the least of the gifts. It might be the least gift according to pastors and leaders who don't want it showing up in their churches, but in the New Testament Church of the Bible, it's an essential tool for edifying believers to fulfill their missions and opens them up to the rest of the gifts. Everyone in my church will be getting a copy of this book.

Nick Champlin

Pastor, Faith Christian Church, Clearwater, FL

CHAPTER 1

THE UNSPEAKABLE VALUE OF PRAYING IN TONGUES

The Holy Spirit said to me up on the inside:

"Many of My people need to be muted and others unmuted."

Stay with me, and I'll explain how the Spirit of God unveiled this statement to me.

First, I must say that the following thoughts are some new, wonderful, and heavenly thoughts about the devotional prayer language the Bible refers to as "tongues." This will not be your basic, foundational teaching that rightly divides the public gift of divers tongues with interpretation from the personal devotional tongues all Spirit-baptized believers should receive. This is not necessarily a new teaching, but these are heightened insights that I've received that I'm willing to submit to leading elders and ministers in the body of Christ and all saints hungry for more of God.

THE LAST DAYS COMPANY CALLING

You see, I'm part of a company of last days preachers who are called to prepare the way of the Lord and make His paths straight. Part of that calling is to help restore certain elements and truths of the work and move of the Holy Spirit back to the body of Christ, lest it be lost to a generation. This is one reason the Lord dealt with me to conduct Holy Ghost Forums, where seasoned ministers can teach and demonstrate the move of the Holy Spirit. Some still think our Forums are just a bless-me time, typical of some Charismatic junkies who always seem to be chasing the sensational. Far from it! It's a school of the Spirit for saints and young ministers to glean and learn from. Some things are better caught than just taught.

Another part of that calling, alongside my wife, is to help restore certain elements of prayer and intercession that must be passed on to the next generation. These two things are an ever-increasing burden in our hearts.

My purpose in writing this book is to motivate you far beyond the so-called seeker-friendly movement that under-emphasized the work and power of the Holy Spirit and greatly devalued the utmost importance of tongues. In my humble, honest opinion, it was one of the greatest crimes against the Holy Spirit in recent times.

SO WHY IS TONGUES SO INVALUABLE?

After all, it has caused so much controversy and division among Christians, so why push the point?

I know not all will receive this, but we need to first understand that God the Father, for the most part, functions on Earth *by invitation*, while maintaining His rights as Creator. In other words, He didn't become involved in my life until a Christian friend and his wife began praying for me, and I decided to surrender my heart to Jesus and give Him control of my life. In other words, I invited Him to be involved in all my affairs. The world is in a mess because it's kicked the living God out. He must be invited back in; if we do that, we will see change in our world.

We have to understand that the Earth has been delegated to man, so a person must make Jesus Lord and invite Him and His Spirit into their life. Yet the Father wants His will to be done on Earth, but man doesn't know how to pray. His knowledge is very limited.

The Father had to find a way to bypass man's *limited* knowledge so that He could impart His *unlimited* knowledge and will into a person, so that person could pray it back to Him, completing the exchange and making it a legal transaction. Do you see that?

For on the Day of Judgment, no human being will be able to bring any accusation against God and blame Him, saying He was not fair and just in all things. All things will be revealed in the end, and God will have been proven faithful and true in all things. So the Father gives a person a language they never learned and fills it with His will, His thoughts, and at times, His own emotions, allowing man to pray it back to Him, thus accomplishing His perfect will on the Earth.

Isn't that just so grand of a plan?

Yet ignorant and misled people fight against this prayer language called "tongues," choosing instead to continue to pray only with their limited knowledge in their own understanding. Actually, that's offensive to God when He has given us a much higher way to pray — a way that bypasses our small intellect and such limited knowledge.

PRAYING CAN BE OFFENSIVE TO GOD

Do you remember how Peter pulled Jesus aside and rebuked Him for telling His disciples that He was going to suffer and be killed?

Notice Jesus' response:

"But Jesus turned away from Peter and said to him, 'Get behind Me, Satan! You are in My way [an offense and a hindrance *and a* snare *to Me]; for you are minding what partakes not of the nature and quality of God, but of men'"* (Matthew 16:23 — AMPC).

What Peter said under the devil's influence was offensive to Jesus! Even so, *many* things we say and pray are offensive to Him. Jesus said that the words Satan spoke through Peter were of the *nature and quality of man.* This is exactly how it is when we pray with only our limited knowledge and refuse the higher way of praying in the Spirit or in tongues. One way can be very soulish and according to our own natural understanding, and the other way is spiritual and according to God's understanding. One is very limited, and the other unlimited. Here's a great verse filled with spiritual truth:

"So too the [Holy] Spirit comes to our aid and bears us up in our weakness; for we do not know what prayer to offer nor how to offer it worthily as we ought, but the Spirit Himself goes to meet our supplication and pleads in our behalf with unspeakable yearnings and groanings too deep for utterance" (Romans 8:26 — AMPC).

This verse basically says that we don't know what or how to pray as we should. But the Spirit aids us or helps us. Here is the definition of *help,* which the King James Version uses:

The Greek word for "help" is very interesting. It is *'synantilambanetai'*, a compound word meaning "to take hold together with us against." Paul said: "The Holy Spirit takes hold together with us against our weakness of not knowing how to pray as we should."

That's so fantastic!

So often we pray amiss because we are not allowing the Holy Spirit to help us. For instance, I can be praying for my brother, a friend, or even someone I don't know, and actually begin to feel the Father's or Jesus' emotions for them, and even weep or laugh in joy, knowing the answer is coming. I know that I've prayed through on the situation — to even actually *understanding,* through interpretation, what I'm praying about and why tongues is so beneficial, and why it feels so good on the inside. I can say, "Father, I pray for my brother or sister this morning," or a sinner, and then go into tongues, knowing I am praying His perfect will for their life this day. We can do this when praying for presidents and governments, or the body of Christ, or any number of things and situations.

Praying only from our soul and with only our own understanding is the big reason our prayers are unfruitful and often ineffective. Those prayers need to be muted. Let us stop praying with only our limited understanding, in mere languages of men, whether it be English or Spanish, or French or Portuguese, and begin utilizing our prayer language of tongues that surpasses our natural mind. Those prayers need to be unmuted. It's a heavenly language. It's kingdom linguistics. It's a higher way.

"Therefore let him who speaks in a tongue pray that he may interpret. For if I pray in a tongue, my spirit prays, but my understanding is unfruitful. What is the conclusion then? I will pray with the spirit, and I will also pray with the understanding. I will sing with the spirit, and I will also sing with the understanding" (1 Corinthians 14:13-15).

Notice that praying with your own understanding should follow praying with your spirit by the Holy Spirit. (The *Amplified Version* brings that out). In other words, the apostle Paul is implying here that we can and should ask God to help us interpret our prayers in the spirit or in tongues, so that our minds can be fruitful. We can cultivate our prayer lives and move into praying with tongues and interpretation. But it's not always necessary because inexperienced Christians are prone to put their own interpretation on it. This must be taught and demonstrated by experienced people of prayer who know how to move in those realms.

There is much more to say about this.

Stay tuned...

CHAPTER 2

TONGUES WINS BATTLES

"For if the trumpet makes an uncertain sound, who will prepare for battle?" (1 Corinthians 14:8).

The apostle Paul likened the clear sound of the trumpet to the correct use of tongues. And by extension, we can say that every Old Testament battle which involved the use of the trumpet hints at the importance of tongues in our New Testament battles — thus echoing the high value of tongues.

In light of this, notice this amazing scripture:

*"Those who built on the wall, and those who carried burdens, loaded themselves so that with one hand they worked at construction, and with the other held a weapon. Every one of the builders had his sword girded at his side as he built. **And the one who sounded the trumpet was beside me**"* (Nehemiah 4:17-18).

Pray-ers should be standing by those who are laboring and fighting on the front lines of ministry and are preaching the Word of God, which is the sword of the Spirit (Ephesians 6:17). Additionally, and more importantly, battles are won and casualties are averted when pray-ers who are watchful are sounding the trumpet and praying much in other tongues.

LOSS OF LIFE AVERTED IN DANGEROUS STORM

I remember hearing a story about one Brother Boley, a missionary to West Africa in the last century. One day he was returning from a missionary trip to one of the islands off the coast. One night, a sister back at the mission station had a great burden to pray. She didn't know what it was about, so she began to pray in tongues. The burden kept increasing until she experienced a lightness in her spirit, and she knew, whatever it was, that she had prayed through. At the end of her prayer time, she saw Brother Boley's face.

Little did she know that, during her time of prayer, Brother Boley's boat was experiencing turbulent waves and heavy winds, and being tossed at sea until his life and those of the others on the boat were in great danger. They didn't have any navigation systems back then, so the boat was at the mercy of the elements.

As the boat drew nearer to shore during the storm, it came up on a coral reef. They were faced with two equally poor options: try to go through the reef and have the boat broken into pieces, or remain out at sea and risk the danger of the boat being capsized and everyone succumbing to an awful death at sea.

They began moving forward, and by a miracle of God, suddenly the boat sailed into the air and landed on the other side of the reef and eventually unto the shore. When the lady compared notes with Brother Boley concerning the exact time of this miraculous deliverance, it was the same time she'd felt the burden lift. She had prayed through to victory, and not a life was lost on that boat. Hallelujah!

This is the extent of what praying in tongues and in the Spirit can do. It can make tremendous power available, dynamic in its working (James 5:16 — AMP). If that sister had just prayed a simple prayer for protection or some soulish thing, the victory would've never come. Thank God for sensitive people who know the touch of the Spirit of God. As you develop sensitivity, you will know when to pray the prayer of petition or faith and when to go further with the prayer of intercession.

The dangers that are averted, the victories that are won, and the breakthroughs that come through this type of praying will be realized only in eternity.

LOSS OF LIFE NOT AVERTED

Another story I remember that did not turn out so well was told by a minister who kept having this impression of his 25-year old niece being thrown from a car. This minister was used by God in prayer, but he got busy and didn't wait on the Lord about this constant impression he was having. All he did was claim divine protection and ask the Lord to keep her safe. In other words, he prayed the prayer of faith (James 5:15). But you see, friends, this is where we can miss it. The Bible instructs us to pray with all kinds of prayer or all manner of prayer (Ephesians

6:18 AMPC), and asking or claiming divine protection is only one way or one kind of praying. Where we often miss it as people of prayer is to rely on petitional praying, or the prayer of asking God for something in faith, when the Spirit of God may be leading us into making further intercession on a situation or on someone's behalf.

This minister found out later that his 25-year old niece had been killed in a tragic car accident. He felt so bad for being insensitive to the Spirit's touch and had to go before the Lord in repentance. Often this is how it is with many careless saints. The Holy Spirit is always looking to lay some prayer burden on someone's heart, but we are either too casual and careless about it, or we are just unfamiliar with the Holy Spirit's leadings. And then ignorant people blame God for tragedies and bad things that happen, but the whole time, the Lord was working to stop it or avert such things. He needs our cooperation.

Remember that I said in the last chapter that God works on Earth *by invitation*. Authority on the Earth was originally delegated to man (Adam), but through sin and the fall of man, Satan stole that authority. This is the reason the devil is called the "*god*" of this world (2 Corinthians 4:3-4). But through the cross Jesus restored that authority back to man, and He has chosen to work legally with man to exercise that authority on Earth once more.

"For he who speaks in a tongue does not speak to men but to God, for no one understands him; however, in the spirit he speaks mysteries" (1 Corinthians 14:2).

Praying forth His mysteries is a huge part of that because we don't know how to pray as we should. Of course, we can pray according to the Word of God as it instructs us, but God has given us His Spirit and a heavenly prayer language that works wonders and gets results. From the aforementioned positive example one can see that there's something about it that releases God's miraculous workings and power.

CHAPTER 3

TONGUES AS A SIGN

In the early 1960s, an American Christian businessman was asked to speak at a business conference in Tokyo, Japan, held by a Christian businessman's organization. The meeting was open to all, and an American Christian, W.E. Deming, who had helped rebuild Japan's industrial capabilities after WW2 using principles found in scripture, was scheduled to be the main speaker. So any business meeting involving Christianity was appealing to business leaders there.

When the man was about to speak, it was explained to him that his interpreter had fallen ill, and they had no one to take his place. Again, this was in the early 1960s, when English was not in as widespread use in Japan as it is today.

The speaker panicked.

The thought of speaking to 2,000 Japanese business leaders in English who wouldn't understand him made him anxious. Instantly the Lord told him: *"Just speak in tongues."* Nervously, he did so, explaining that he started out in his prayer language, but then it quickly changed into what proved to be Japanese.

After nearly an hour, it trickled off, and the man stopped speaking. Suddenly, more than 200 Japanese businessmen rushed toward the platform, and just as suddenly, the Holy Spirit came on them, and they began speaking in tongues.

Testimonies like these abound, and it is clear that, just as it was on the day of Pentecost, when the 120 spoke in languages they had never learned but others understood, these things still happen today.

A COUPLE OF PERSONAL EXPERIENCES

A few years ago, I had a similar experience praying with a tribal man in Africa who also spoke some English, and who was actually my interpreter. While I was using the bathroom, I continued to pray out loud, when suddenly my tongue changed, and apparently, unbeknownst to me, I began speaking this man's native dialect. He overheard me and was amazed and told me that it was a meaningful message from God to him in his own native dialect concerning his calling.

I've heard similar stories like these throughout my life and have concluded that the miracle is not always in the speaker but in the hearer. Through a miracle, God makes them to hear the message in their own language.

*"And there were dwelling in Jerusalem Jews, devout men, from every nation under heaven. And when this sound occurred, the multitude came together, and were confused, because everyone **HEARD** them speak in his own language. Then they were all amazed and marveled, saying to one another, 'Look, are not all these who speak Galileans? And how is it that we **HEAR**, each in our own language in which we were born? Parthians and Medes and Elamites, those dwelling in Mesopotamia, Judea and Cappadocia, Pontus and Asia, Phrygia and Pamphylia, Egypt and the parts of Libya adjoining Cyrene, visitors from Rome, both Jews and proselytes, Cretans and Arabs — we **HEAR** them speaking in our own tongues the wonderful works of God.' So they were all amazed and perplexed, saying to one another, 'Whatever could this mean?'" (Acts 2:5-12).*

There was another similar instance of this when we were missionaries living in the Islamic nation of Gambia. My wife, Carolyn, and I were praying in the Spirit or in other tongues with our staff one morning, and she kept hearing me say the word "Muhammed." But I wasn't saying "Muhammed" but only praying in tongues. After waiting on the Lord for His direction in the matter, He led us to address the spirit of Muhammed that apparently was a principality in that nation. Shortly thereafter, incredible miracles and healings started happening, and we began seeing a real breakthrough and change in the nation and our ministry.

You can't do this in the flesh, folks, like so many do today. You can't manufacture names of principalities and demon powers and just address them. It has to be done in the Spirit and at the leading of the Lord.

CHAPTER 4

TONGUES FOR PERSONAL EDIFICATION

As you can see and have read, there are different purposes and uses of tongues. You can't just put them all in the same bag, or you'll be hopelessly confused. This is another reason for such controversy concerning tongues. Poor teaching. Poor learning. Poor understanding.

So far, we've touched upon the use of tongues for prayer and intercession, tongues as a sign when people understand or hear the tongue in their own language. We will also touch upon the public gift of divers tongues requiring interpretation, as well as on cultivating an ability to interpret our own prayers.

But in this chapter, I'd like to put an emphasis on the most basic use of tongues — as a means of personal edification and the building up of our spirits — while touching also upon the privilege of interpreting our private prayers.

I have made a private practice of praying in tongues or *"speaking mysteries"* (1 Corinthians 14:2) extensively for more than 40 years now. I sincerely believe this is an important part of why I've been able to fulfill God's plan for my life. So what I'm sharing comes not only from the Word of God but also from personal experience.

I've also made a practice of singing with my spirit in tongues and interpreting those songs with beautiful words in my own understanding. I have a collection of these psalms, and hymns, and spiritual songs (Ephesians 5:19; Colossians 3:16) that I've kept in a journal for many years. Here is one song that describes the dimension of edification we experience when we pray or sing with our spirits.

When I sing in the Spirit, I go higher,

When I sing in the Spirit, I soar to higher heights,

Above this realm of the physical senses,

My spirit is edified...

High, higher, highest,

High, higher, highest,

I'm moving from one degree to another,

I'm being trained in heaven's praise,

For I have an unction from the Holy One.

Now the casual reader or listener may not discern the spiritual nature of those simple verses (and there was a melody to it that has stuck with me all these years), but it is freighted with the Spirit of God. The words were not rehearsed or composed — they came by the inspiration of the Holy Spirit in interpretation. If you've been baptized with the Holy Spirit, you have an unction from Him that teaches you, not in the words of human wisdom but in the higher wisdom that comes from the anointing of the Holy Spirit.

"For what man knows the things of a man except the spirit of the man which is in him? Even so no one knows the things of God except the Spirit of God. Now we have received, not the spirit of the world, but the Spirit who is from God, that we might know the things that have been freely given to us by God. These things we also speak, not in words which man's wisdom teaches but which the Holy Spirit teaches, comparing spiritual things with spiritual." (1 Corinthians 2:11-13)

As the aforementioned song says, we are edified above this realm of the physical senses when we sing or pray in the Spirit. Singing *of* the Lord and *to* the Lord keeps you full, fresh, and free.

Our prayers in the Spirit work virtually the same way as singing in the Spirit. Let me explain.

When I spend long times just praying in tongues, I will begin to know inwardly some of what I am praying about. I'll begin to sense it and interpret it in English at times, so that my understanding becomes fruitful. I also love to sing in tongues, and the same basic thing begins to happen. I will usually start to hear a word or two, or a phrase, or a title to a psalm, a song, or a hymn. This is perfectly in line with the Scriptures, which command us to be filled with the Spirit by speaking or singing.

"And do not be drunk with wine, in which is dissipation; but be filled with the Spirit, speaking to one another in psalms and hymns and spiritual songs, singing and making melody in your heart to the Lord..." (Ephesians 5:18-19)

The more you pray in tongues, the more you fine-tune your spirit. You become more familiar with the interpretation processes of the Holy Spirit, and your faith is developed in prophecy. Paul said this:

"Therefore let him who speaks in a tongue pray that he may interpret. For if I pray in a tongue, my spirit prays, but my understanding is unfruitful. What is the conclusion then? I will pray with the spirit, and I will also pray with the understanding. I will sing with the spirit, and I will also sing with the understanding." (1 Corinthians 14:13-15)

Paul prayed and sang with the spirit, or in tongues, and then interpreted with his understanding what he prayed or sang. He exhorts those who speak in tongues to also pray for interpretation. That's a good place to start.

LIKE HINDS FEET

Here is a neat little scripture tucked into the minor prophet's book that bears his name. It is a type and shadow of praying with interpretation.

"The Lord God is my strength; He will make my feet like hind's feet, and he will make me walk upon mine high places" (Habakkuk 3:19 — KJV).

A doe or a deer's hind feet will often fill their front tracks, landing virtually in the same place, so that only one set of tracks appears. My understanding is that it's not quite the same way with a buck's tracks. Bucks often appear to do a very slight under step due to the hind feet being shorter.

The analogy here is that this is the effect that praying in the Spirit or in tongues with interpretation has. You will then be able to walk on your prayers.

"He will make me walk upon mine high places."

But it's not always necessary to interpret your own prayer language. You are edifying yourself either way and speaking or praying forth mysteries concerning the plans and purposes of God. You are building a highway in the Spirit that you can ride on. Unfortunately and sadly, that cannot be said of believers who only pray with their understanding and intellect. They might build a dirt road or a path through the wilderness, but building a highway is so much better and faster.

Saints who intentionally and consistently utilize their prayer language have a much better chance to maximize the effect of their prayers and fulfill the plan and purpose of God for their lives. By praying much in the Spirit and in other tongues, they gain a great advantage and place their lives on the fast track of God's perfect will for their lives and in the lives of those they pray for.

Moreover, the more you pray in tongues, the more you edify yourself. Speaking and singing under the inspiration of the Holy Spirit also edifies you and fills you. It's a wonderful life on Earth to always minister from a place of edification.

Smith Wigglesworth, the great apostle of faith from the last century, said that he'd edify himself in the afternoon by praying a couple of hours in tongues and then go out at night and edify the people through his preaching. I've made a practice of that in my own life and ministry also.

"He who speaks in a tongue edifies himself..." (1 Corinthians 14:4a).

"Edify" means "to build yourself up."

"But you, beloved, building yourselves up on your most holy faith, praying in the Holy Spirit, keep yourselves in the love of God, looking for the mercy of our Lord Jesus Christ unto eternal life" (Jude 20-21).

Notice the expression, *"building yourself up on your most holy faith by praying in the Holy Spirit."* You don't receive faith when you pray in tongues, because faith comes by hearing the Word of God (Romans 10:17), but the faith you already have is stimulated when you pray in tongues. Something happens on the inside that is sometimes difficult to explain. Your spirit ascends as your mind grows quiet. The will of God becomes clearer to you. Peace takes over in troubling situations. Revelation comes. Direction is given. Oh, what we miss when we don't edify ourselves by praying in the Spirit or in tongues!

A PERSONAL TESTIMONY OF INDULGING IN TONGUES

In the winter of 2001-2002, I was led into a season of praying excessively in other tongues. After many days, I began to hear beautiful words as the Holy Spirit began to expound on God's plan concerning my character and calling. It became like a precious scroll to me that fed and fueled my spirit. I ate that scroll, and it satisfied me.

"And He said to me, 'Son of man, feed your belly, and fill your stomach with this scroll that I give you.' So I ate, and it was in my mouth like honey in sweetness" (Ezekiel 3:3).

This is what happens when the revelation and interpretation come after praying in the Spirit at length and making it a consistent practice in your life. You will open up your life and spirit to the teaching of the Holy Spirit.

"These things we also speak, not in words which man's wisdom teaches but which the Holy Spirit teaches, comparing spiritual things with spiritual" (1 Corinthians 2:12-13).

Again, I must reiterate that the revelation in those words didn't come until after many hours and days of praying in tongues. My tongues were a mystery until God unveiled the revelation of it through interpretation. God wants every one of His children to enjoy this privilege. It's a sweet life. It's the best life! This is the reason these scriptures admonish the saints to pray that they would interpret their private speaking or praying in tongues in the Spirit.

"Therefore let him who speaks in a tongue pray that he may interpret. For if I pray in a tongue, my spirit prays, but my understanding is unfruitful. What is the conclusion then? I will pray with the spirit, and I will also pray with the understanding. I will sing with the spirit, and I will also sing with the understanding" (1 Corinthians 14:13-15).

The apostle Paul is telling us to pray with our spirits and with our understanding also. He is implying that what we pray with our spirits, we should interpret with our understanding. You see, you can start praying with your spirit in tongues and then move into the interpretation of it with your understanding, which is the best way. But you could also begin praying with your understanding and trust the Holy Spirit to give you utterance to take you on into tongues and praying more with your spirit. We will be expounding more on this in another chapter.

It's difficult to explain spiritual things to the natural man. But often times you can be praying hours in tongues, and there might be a one or two-word interpretation given to you, or an entire chapter of words that the Holy Ghost teaches. The latter was the case with me in this season. By the end of that winter, I had many pages written in document form of the revelation the Lord unveiled to me concerning my life and calling. I included much of it in a book I published years ago called, *A Journal Of A Journey To His Holiness.* It contains wisdom that has helped many readers to apply to their lives as well.

The possibility also exists that you won't receive any interpretation of what you're praying or speaking in tongues in a mystery. It's not always necessary. Just know and be assured that, when you're praying or singing in the Spirit, you are building up yourself and edifying yourself above this realm of the physical senses, and making great advances in the Spirit concerning your life and calling.

ONE CAUTION: LET THE WORD DWELL IN YOU RICHLY

To maintain accuracy in your prayer life, you must stick and stay with the Word of God, especially if you want to develop a life of praise and worship in the Spirit and minister to the Lord supernaturally in psalms, hymns, and spiritual songs.

"Let the word of Christ dwell in you richly in all wisdom, teaching and admonishing one another in psalms and hymns and spiritual songs, singing with grace in your hearts to the Lord" (Colossians 3:16).

The more you saturate yourself with the Word of God, the more the Holy Spirit can draw it out of you, especially during hard times and trials when you most need the encouragement. It's just like putting money in the bank. No deposits. No withdrawals. Believers who are saturated with the Word of God make the best candidates to minister to themselves and to others in Spirit-inspired psalms, hymns, and spiritual songs. It's the Word of God and the scriptures that have the power to minister to our spirits.

As a New Testament example, while in prison and in pain, Paul and Silas prayed and then sang praises unto God (Acts 16:25). As an Old Testament example, David would often sing and praise God in times of trouble and trial. The book of Psalms is filled with the Spirit-inspired praises of David. For example, in Ziklag, when David's men spoke of stoning him because their enemies had burned their city, destroyed their houses, and kidnapped their families, notice what David did in this severe trial.

"Now David was greatly distressed, for the people spoke of stoning him, because the soul of all the people was grieved, every man for his sons and his daughters. But David strengthened (encouraged) himself in the Lord his God" (1 Samuel 30:6).

I'm sure it was in times like these when David would minister to the Lord in praise. That is one of the great ways to encourage yourself in the Lord. Again, the

Psalms are full of such praise and thanksgiving. Notice this verse, and meditate on it in light of your trials.

"Is anyone among you suffering? Let him pray. Is anyone cheerful? Let him sing psalms" (James 5:13).

The suffering here is a result of being afflicted in a trial. The two aforementioned examples of Paul and Silas in prison, and David in Ziklag would most definitely apply. They first prayed and then became cheerful as they entered into praise and rejoicing in the Spirit. Can you see that from the aforementioned scripture verse?

This is the way into personal edification and living a Spirit-filled victorious life. Under the new covenant, we have a greater advantage of being Spirit-filled and utilizing our prayer language of tongues to pray and sing in the Spirit and then with our understanding.

Remember, you are the primary steward of your own personal edification. You can grumble and complain and focus on the negativity and adversity that life brings us all, or you can choose to rejoice in the Spirit and edify yourself above it all.

CHAPTER 5

DIVERS TONGUES AND INTERPRETATION OF TONGUES

Back toward the first half of the last century, there was an abundance of the public use of tongues with interpretation. Today, there is so little manifestation of it. The reason is a lack of teaching, demonstration, and emphasis. It is something we must recover.

There are nine gifts or manifestations of the Holy Spirit (1 Corinthians 12:7-11). Seven of the nine were operative under the ministry of the prophets in the Old Testament. The other two were reserved for the saints of the New Testament dispensation. Those two that Jesus left us were *"divers tongues"* and *"interpretation of tongues."* The word *"divers"* (or *"diverse"*) simply means that it's more than just your regular devotional tongues that every believer should have upon receiving the baptism with the Holy Spirit. Divers tongues is deeper and more articulate. *"Divers"* means different kinds of tongues.

There's an unction and a quickening on it with an interpretation that should follow. The Bible talks about *"tongues of men"* and *"tongues of angels"* (1 Corinthians 13:1). When you hear *"divers tongues,"* it sounds almost angelic because there is a higher anointing on it. In other words, it's not your regular prayer and devotional tongue. It's a gift and a manifestation of the Spirit for public use.

* In the English language of the 17th century — the century in which the Bible was translated definitively into English from its original Hebrew, Greek, and Latin versions — the word "diverse" was spelled "divers." But in modern English, this spelling is considered archaic and is no longer used [*ed.*] The older King James Version uses "divers." The New King James actually uses "different" kinds of tongues.

PRIVATE TONGUES IS NOT A GIFT

Many Christians often refer to the private use of tongues as "a gift," but that is not exactly right. The New Testament never calls the private use of tongues that every believer should receive "a gift." The gift is the Holy Spirit.

"Then Peter said to them, 'Repent, and let every one of you be baptized in the name of Jesus Christ for the remission of sins; and you shall receive the gift of the Holy Spirit'" (Acts 2:38).

One of the Holy Spirit's nine manifestations is *divers* tongues. *Divers* tongues is considered a gift or a manifestation of the Holy Spirit, but your devotional tongue is not.

I believe the twin gifts of tongues and interpretation to be the signature gifts of the New Testament. They are the two gifts Jesus specifically left for His glorious Church. Many count them as the lesser gifts and place them on the bottom, but they are the crown jewels and should be placed at the top. These two gifts are more likely to be initiated by us under the inspiration of the Holy Spirit than any other. When it comes to the power gifts (faith, gifts of healing, and working of miracles) and the revelation gifts (word of knowledge, word of wisdom, and discerning of spirits), you can't really manufacture the anointing for those gifts. In other words, you can't anoint yourself with power or give yourself a revelation, but you can stir yourself up in the vocal gifts. Why do you think those three gifts of divers tongues, interpretation of tongues, and prophecy were the most common in the early Church meetings (1 Corinthians 14)? Because they are more initiated by believers, as they are filled with the Spirit than any other gift (For more on these twin gifts, refer to author's book *Shaping Local Churches For The Move Of The Holy Spirit*).

A UNIQUE ASPECT OF THE MINISTRY OF TONGUES AND INTERPRETATION

In conclusion, I'd like to bring out another unique element or aspect of divers tongues and interpretation of tongues, that we especially find in the ministry of the prophets.

"I have also spoken by the prophets, and have multiplied visions; I have given <u>*symbols*</u> *through the witness of the prophets"* (Hosea 12:10).

The word "symbols" is also translated "parables".

Prophets and anointed ministers, or any saint the Spirit of God anoints, to move in tongues and interpretation of tongues, may occasionally act out the message being given in tongues. In other words, if the one giving a tongue, demonstrates in a symbol or a particular gesture of some kind the message being given, a good interpreter will pick that up in the Spirit and be able to interpret it the same way — using the same symbols or gestures. This can be demonstrated in varied forms. For example, among the symbols by which the prophets demonstrated God's message was the life of Hosea himself and his relationship with his wife Gomer, intended to depict God's love for Israel.

Although the twin gifts of divers tongues and interpretation of tongues were not manifested in the Old Testament, prophecy and the gifts of revelation (word of wisdom, word of knowledge, and discerning of spirits) were, and often a prophet would demonstrate or dramatize the message.

The New Testament example of this would be Agabus using Paul's belt to demonstrate the persecution he would experience in Jerusalem.

*"On the next day we who were Paul's companions departed and came to Caesarea, and entered the house of Philip the evangelist, who was one of the seven, and stayed with him. Now this man had four virgin daughters who prophesied. And as we stayed many days, a certain prophet named Agabus came down from Judea. **When he had come to us, he took Paul's belt, bound his own hands and feet, and said, 'Thus says the Holy Spirit, So shall the Jews at Jerusalem bind the man who owns this belt, and deliver him into the hands of the Gentiles'"** (Acts 21:8-11).*

Now this message from Agabus could've been given just through straight prophecy or even tongues and interpretation. It doesn't really say. But the point is that there was some symbolism and a gesture given to show forth the message God was giving to Paul and those present. I have witnessed this type of ministry many times through our panel of ministers in our Holy Ghost Forums. My wife and I have also been used by the Lord this way a number of times through the years. It's a beautiful and marvelous way to show forth what the Lord may be saying to His people.

Mom and Dad Goodwin, who pastored a church in Pasadena, Texas in the 1950s and 60s, were prolific in this ministry. Customarily, Mom would speak out a message in divers tongues, physically demonstrating and acting out the gist of the message. Dad would then follow, by interpreting the message into English, repeating the same physical actions, gestures, and mannerisms. This was God's way of dramatizing the message.

I remember reading one of many examples of this ministry operating through them. One time Mom took a handkerchief in her hand and began uttering a message in tongues while twisting the handkerchief. She then threw the handkerchief on the floor. Continuing to speak in tongues, she picked up the handkerchief, put it on her arm, and began to rub it. Dad then gave the interpretation: "I could take you like an old rag, wring you out, and throw you down. But I don't treat My people that way. Instead, when they are down, I pick them up, place them on my arm, and caress them as a mother does her baby."

Isn't that a beautiful characterization of our Father God? The words alone are wonderful, but the message was made even more compelling by being acted out before the people. This is a ministry that needs to be restored today in the Church to bless and edify the body of Christ.

CHAPTER 6

SPIRITUAL TRAVAIL AND GROANINGS

"My little children, for whom I travail in birth again until Christ is formed in you..." (Galatians 4:19).

Twice the apostle Paul travailed and made spiritual intercession for these Galatian Christians. Note the word *"again"*. He travailed for them to be born again and then for their spiritual growth. Paul had taught them the Word of God, but, apparently, they were not growing in grace. Christ was not being formed in them. Instead of moving forward in Christ, they wanted to revert back to the Law.

You see, sometimes just teaching the Word alone will not cause Christ to be formed in young believers. Spiritual travail and intercession are needed. I believe this spiritual travail and groaning in the Spirit to be an extension of praying in other tongues and making intercession for things we do not know exactly how to pray for.

"Likewise the Spirit also helps in our weaknesses. For we do not know what we should pray for as we ought, but the Spirit Himself makes intercession for us with groanings which cannot be uttered" (Romans 8:26).

These groanings escape your lips because they are your groanings and not the Holy Spirit's groanings. It's a form of spiritual travail and giving birth to souls, or anything else the Lord wants us to give birth to. Notice these verses:

"Who hath heard such a thing? Who hath seen such things? Shall the earth be made to bring forth in one day? Or shall a nation be born at once? For as soon as Zion travailed, she brought forth her children. 'Shall I bring to the birth, and not cause to bring forth?' saith the Lord. 'Shall I cause to bring forth, and shut the womb?' saith thy God" (Isaiah 66:8-9).

Very often, the Old Testament prophets prophesied of the rebirth of Israel, but many times there was a twofold application — both the natural and spiritual. In this scripture, the spiritual application is stronger. Zion is symbolic of the Church and all those who believe in Christ (Hebrews 12:18-24; esp. v. 22).

You can travail for sinners and for saints. When a woman gives birth to a child, she groans and travails. The reason sometimes many conversions don't amount to anything is that they were not new births but only decisions.

Paul travailed for these Galatians to be born again and then for Christ to be formed in them. They were babes in Christ and needed to grow. Until Christ is formed in a new believer, he will naturally continue to do things that are wrong, even though he may be born again and filled with the Spirit.

There's a similarity between physical growth and spiritual growth. No one is born a full-grown human. As ministers, we are to teach believers the Word of God, but also prayer and travail must be prevalent for their spiritual growth and for Christ to be formed in them.

The same thing holds true with being born again. Some sinners will be born again from simply hearing and believing the truth of the gospel and responding to it. But others will never be truly born again until someone makes spiritual intercession for them. Only intercession in the Spirit will break the power of Satan over them and set them free. Intercession in the Spirit overpowers the works of the devil that hold people in bondage, very often against their will, where they can't make the right decision. Spiritual intercession and travail work to the pulling down of strongholds.

The same is true with sick and diseased people. Some will be healed by believing the Word of God, or by a manifestation of the Spirit, but others will not be healed until spiritual intercession is made for them. At times a true intercessor will even take on the same symptoms in the Spirit as the sick and diseased one they are praying for. I know of a mighty intercessor who has seen hundreds of sick/diseased people healed through this form of intercession.

This same principles of soul travail and intercessory prayer for lost souls and the sick and diseased are also involved in other things. For example, very often, before a ministry or a church or a move of God can come into full bloom, there will have to be some travail to give birth to it. Many ministries and churches are running ahead of their prayers.

I heard of one woman in Texas back in the early part of the last century who had a real ministry in prayer and soul travail, for churches to be birthed in the region where she lived. Through soul travail and intercessory prayer, she would pray a church into every town in her region that didn't already have a full gospel church until one was raised up. That is a lost art in today's modern church. Instead, we now have so-called "prophets" who go into regions and claim to shift the atmosphere through their prophetic declarations until revival supposedly breaks out. If that were true, then America and the nations would be burning with revival right now. But unfortunately, and sadly, that's not the case. Often, it's this kind of prayer and soul travail that brings these things forth and gives birth to the move of God.

It's not just one man's prayers that are going to do the job — it's going to take the body of Christ to do it. Many intercessors can come to the edge of giving birth but never do. Why? Because it requires more perseverance and help from others.

One seasoned man of prayer stated that sometimes it feels like a large body of water like the Pacific Ocean is right above us, and, if someone would pull a certain lever, that water would come flowing down and bless us all. There's a body of blessing above us, but we must pray this way and give birth to it before God pours it out. Just as the prince of Persia (Satan) hindered the prayers of Daniel in the second heaven, so it is today. However, Daniel's words were heard the first day he prayed.

"Then he said to me, 'Do not fear, Daniel, for from the first day that you set your heart to understand, and to humble yourself before your God, your words were heard; and I have come because of your words. But the prince of the kingdom of Persia withstood me twenty-one days; and behold, Michael, one of the chief princes, came to help me, for I had been left alone there with the kings of Persia'" (Daniel 10:12-13).

It's not God that is holding back our prayers — it is Satanic forces. Through intercessory prayer, we can win the victory if we will persevere.

How much more is this true under the New Covenant? The holy blood of Jesus has been shed. The Holy Spirit has been poured out. Satan has been defeated and stripped of his authority. We now have our supernatural prayer language of tongues and the authority to wield the sword of the Spirit, the Word of God, and use the Name of Jesus. We are called to execute Satan's defeat through this kind of prayer and intercession.

There's been a renewed emphasis on prayer in this generation, but so often we fall short of making real spiritual intercession and soul travail. Too many prayers are offered only with our limited understanding instead of in the Spirit in other tongues and with groanings and travail.

CHAPTER 7

DEEPER BAPTISMS WITH THE HOLY SPIRIT

"And for three days he was without sight, and neither ate nor drank" (Acts 9:9 — ESV).

There is something about this verse I can't get away from. The dealings of God in a man can be unusual and against our carnal thinking and traditional ways. Let me ask you something.

Have you ever gone three days without food and drink and just stayed still in one general place with little to no activity? If not, then how do you know what's on the other side of that?

A friend of mine (Brian) was supernaturally delivered from alcohol and drug addiction because he went on a three-day fast with no food and no water. Even when brushing his teeth, he would spit the water out. When his doctor heard he was free of drugs and alcohol, he cleared his schedule for the day just to sit with Brian. He wanted to know how he did it without ever experiencing withdrawals. Brian attributed it to the three-day fast with no food or water. Praise God!

I've been on longer fasts at times, especially in my youth, but I was taught to drink lots of water when fasting. Naturally, that is sound advice. Water is a healing agent, with many benefits to your body. But if you go through the Scriptures, there is a pattern of the three-day fast, which I've always known but never paid much attention to the "without water" part. I just always thought it was unhealthy and not really the best for your body.

In Esther 4:16, we find Esther exhorting Mordecai to persuade the Jews to fast.

"Neither eat nor drink for three days, night or day."

No drink. No water.

This was clearly in preparation for her highly risky attempt to see the king. It was a time of preparation.

THE HOUSE OF CORNELIUS: ACTS 10

When the Lord opened the door for the gospel to go forth to the Gentiles, he prepared both Cornelius and Peter to meet.

"And Cornelius said, 'Four days ago I was fasting until this hour'" (Acts 10:30a).

For three days, Cornelius had been fasting. Now it was the fourth day, when the Lord visited him and sent an angel to deliver an incredible message, by which Cornelius prepared his household to receive from Peter. It doesn't say what kind of fast it was, but, in the Scriptures, I believe three days without food is the most common fast.

After this preparation in Cornelius's house and also in Peter's heart on the rooftop (Acts 10:9-16), imagine the anticipation and expectation that were present upon Peter's arrival. As a result, here is what happened:

"While Peter yet spake these words, the Holy Ghost fell on all them which heard the word" (Acts 10:44 KJV).

They couldn't wait for him to finish preaching. Their anticipation was so great and their expectation so high.

This is the first time any Gentiles had ever received the baptism with the Holy Ghost. The Jews who were with Peter were astonished when they heard them speak with tongues and magnify God.

A PREPARATION OF THE HEART AND LIFE

This is my conviction. Just as there was a preparation of the hearts of Cornelius and those he gathered in his house, as well as Peter's own heart, there is a preparation of the heart and the life that is necessary for what is coming. Just think of Paul. Picture yourself blind, without sight, and nothing entering your mouth for three full days. Can you imagine the deep work the Lord began doing in Paul and can do in you! What an introduction Paul had to kingdom life! What a way to purge him of all his religiosity and destructive reasonings of thinking Christians were the enemy of God. What a fearful encounter to the beginning of a glorious transformation in the life of Paul! And all this, after seeing a bright light and hearing God's voice on the road to Damascus.

There is so much in Paul's encounter. The Light from heaven! The audible voice of Jesus! Falling to the ground! Having his eyes open but not being able to see! And he was given time to process it all. He trembled and was astonished. Then direction came from the Lord to go to the city and wait (Acts 9:1-9).

All this was followed by Ananias's vision and Spirit-directed visit to minister sight and the baptism with the Holy Spirit to Paul (Saul), and then water baptism (Acts 9:10-18).

THE SUPERNATURAL IN THE EARLY CHURCH

The activities of the Early Church were supernatural — prayer, visions, the gifts of the Holy Spirit, hearing from heaven, and such Divine activity. It was all a part of the way the glorious Church began.

Have you ever noticed, in the book of Acts, how visions and supernatural communication were always in conjunction with prayer? Saul was praying; he had a vision. Ananias was praying; he had a vision (Acts 9). Revelation and direction were given.

Cornelius was praying; he had a vision. Peter was praying; he had a vision (Acts 10). Revelation and direction were given. We see this throughout the book of Acts. The Holy Spirit was active because they prayed in the Spirit.

Besides the deep preparation of hearts, we see here in these two accounts of Paul and Cornelius and Peter in Acts 9 and 10, the other takeaway is that this is often the missing ingredient in getting people baptized with the Holy Spirit — the preparation of the heart! Faith and expectation. A full consecration. A full surrender. A separation from the world. Single-mindedness. Fasting accelerates this process.

Concerning the baptism with the Holy Spirit, although many individuals receive wonderful anointings of the Spirit, some do need instruction on how to yield their tongue to receive their prayer language, but we often get the cart before the horse when it comes to new converts. In other words, it is important that spiritual things are made real to them and that there is a depth of consecration and hunger in their hearts to receive the power of the Holy Spirit. They should know something about the meaning of the baptism and develop a definite hunger and expectation for it instead of being pushed along too fast. Saul had a tremendous conversion experience on the road to Damascus and was blinded and did not eat or drink anything for three days. He also had a heavenly vision. Now granted, we are not all converted the same way, but the principle remains the same.

It is also true that, once we are saved, there is no need to wait or tarry for the Holy Spirit, but the new convert or long-waiting saint may need a vision for it and a clear understanding, faith, and expectation built into his heart. As with all spiritual blessings, including healing, it is important that the heart be thoroughly prepared to receive. Carnal believers will usually have a difficult time receiving the Holy Spirit baptism. Sincere repentance is a prerequisite.

Faith, spiritual hunger, heart preparation, and consecration in the seeking saint are the definite ingredients that multiply our efforts in ministering this sacred baptism to them.

ACTS 2, ACTS 13 — THE SAME

What were they doing in Acts 2 before the initial outpouring of the Spirit? Praying. Waiting. With anticipation. With faith and expectation. They heard from the Lord. They knew they were in the right place at the right time, obeying what the Lord said.

What were they doing in Acts 13:1-3? Seeking. Waiting on

the Lord. Fasting. We don't know how long it was, but again, the results were phenomenal. Those ministers had to be sensing change.

For Peter to have gone up to the housetop to pray in Acts 10 was not in sync with his temperament. At lunchtime? C'mon! There is no way the impetuous

Peter would be praying when it was time to eat! *Ha-ha!* He had a burden! He was sensing change. That's why he was on that rooftop.

GET READY, MAKE ROOM

This is where we are, people, as the body of Christ. Great change is coming — and even now, it is here. Those who are spiritually minded can sense it. It's high time for the deep preparation of our hearts and lives. Only our full consecration is required for a greater deluge of the Spirit's workings and power. Heaven will come and respond to the sincerity of our hearts.

Get ready. Make room for Him.

Three days of being still. Without food and drink. Don't talk much. I guarantee travail will come. Groanings will manifest through you if you'll persevere.

I propose we start there. Fruit will abound.

*** **Disclaimer: If you have any health issues you should check with your health professional before attempting a fast of this kind.**

CHAPTER 8

SPIRITUAL ACCURACY AND EFFECTIVENESS IN PRAYER

I'm going to say something very strong here that I made mention of in an earlier chapter:

Our prayers can actually be offensive to the Lord.

What we say to the Lord or what we pray can actually be offensive because the words are of our own mind and motives and not the will of God. This happens often when we only pray with our own understanding and not in the Spirit. It's difficult to pray amiss when you pray in tongues and in the Spirit.

Paul wrote that he prayed with the Spirit and with understanding, too. He also sang that way. As I stated before, this implies that what he prayed or sang with the Spirit, he interpreted with his understanding. Plainly said, we should do much of our praying with our spirits or in tongues, and ask God to help us interpret our prayers.

The other day my son Daniel and I filled in a two-hour prayer block at our local church, and the Holy Spirit gave me so much utterance and interpretation in prayer and praise that the two hours seemed like fifteen minutes. This is how it is with prayer in the Spirit. You lose a certain consciousness of time. If you pray with only your own understanding, you are greatly limiting the effect and impact of your prayers. After all, what do we know of the mind of God except what is revealed to us by the Holy Spirit? Praying in the Spirit is praying with God's understanding, which is unlimited. Saying or praying words only in our own understanding can actually be offensive to God and get in God's way of what He really desires to accomplish.

Let's look at this scripture again that we noted in Chapter 1.

"Then Peter took Him aside to speak to Him privately and began to reprove and charge Him sharply, saying, 'God forbid, Lord! This must never happen to You!'

"But Jesus turned away from Peter and said to him, 'Get behind Me, Satan! You are in My way [an offense and a hindrance and a snare to Me]; for you are minding what partakes not of the nature and quality of God, but of men'" (Matthew 16:22-23 — AMPC).

When Jesus began speaking the will of the Father that He was to be crucified and killed on the cross and then raised from the dead, Peter actually took Him aside and rebuked Him. Jesus rebuked Satan, who was speaking through Peter, with these words: *"You are an offense unto Me."*

As we've already stated, what Peter said was offensive to Jesus. It is the same way with us when we say things or pray things that are not the will of God. Personal opinions and personal agendas tainted with our own motives and clouded with our own thinking and mental understanding can be offensive to the Lord and grievous to the Spirit of God. This is why He gave us a prayer language, so our prayers could bypass our limited intellect and be acceptable to God. I'll say it again: Praying only with our own mental understanding can be clouded with our own selfish motives.

"Yet you do not have because you do not ask. You ask and do not receive, because you ask amiss, that you may spend it on your pleasures" (James 4:2b-3).

Praying in tongues has been called "the perfect prayer," and, when interpretation accompanies it, our understanding becomes fruitful. But we don't always need interpretation. We can pray in tongues in faith, believing we are praying the perfect will of God — and believing things we simply don't know about.

For example, there can be an ambulance driving by in a haste to transport an injured or a dying person to the hospital, and you could pray with your spirit in tongues the perfect will of God for that precious person, whom you don't know or have never even seen. What a privilege to invite God through prayer into that situation! We are to pray for all saints in the same way.

"...praying always with all prayer and supplication in the Spirit, being watchful to this end with all perseverance and supplication for all the saints*"* (Ephesians 6:18).

How can we possibly pray for *all* saints if we don't know them? It can be done only "*in the Spirit.*"

I remember hearing about one of the early pioneers of the Pentecostal movement, in the early 1900s, before there was any organization among them. They had to communicate in the Spirit. The Holy Spirit told this one pioneer pastor to go over to another church in another state to raise up a young pastor who was dying.

Sometimes we can become so organized that we organize the Holy Spirit right out of our lives and prayer times.

The two ingredients we need to have an effective prayer life is a knowledge of the Word and a knowledge and sensitivity to the Holy Spirit.

For example, the Word of God instructs us on certain things to pray for (I've included quite a few in the last chapter). And it's perfectly fine to pray with your own understanding and intellect about those things. God's will is contained within His Word. For instance, God tells us to pray for our government and kings and all in authority (1 Timothy 2:1-4). But praying only with our intellect and understanding can still fall so short because we don't know all that's facing these governments and authorities behind the scenes. That's where praying in the Spirit comes in, because we don't always know how to pray as we ought.

"So too the [Holy] Spirit comes to our aid and bears us up in our weakness; for we do not know what prayer to offer nor how to offer it worthily as we ought, but the Spirit Himself goes to meet our supplication and pleads in our behalf with unspeakable yearnings and groanings too deep for utterance" (Romans 8:26 — AMPC).

Not all praying is necessarily spiritual. We can make mental intercession, but, without the Spirit's help, it falls so short. We need to pray both ways, but God especially wants us to make spiritual intercession and supplication. For the most part, the Church has failed because it has endeavored to carry out the work of God with only one kind of praying. Mental praying alone is insufficient.

Outside of the few prayers that are outlined in the New Testament, such as the Ephesian prayers (Ephesians 1:16-23; 3:14-21), among several others, it's nearly impossible in our own human reasoning to know what to pray for as we ought. For instance, I know about my own personal life and what to pray for, or even how to pray, but I don't know about others. In Ephesians 6:18, it talks about praying for all saints. I don't know all the saints. Praying for our own personal needs is about as far as most Christians' prayer lives go. Praying only for our individual needs is very limited praying. Even to pray, "God bless so and so" is sort of shallow and quite inadequate. We need the Holy Spirit and our prayer language to be effective in prayer. Perhaps the greatest benefit of being filled with the Holy Ghost is our prayer life. Not only does it benefit you, but we can be a greater blessing and benefit to the Church and the world.

P. C. Nelson, a fine Greek scholar, said that the end of Romans 8:26 reads this way: "*with groanings which cannot be uttered in articulate speech*" (which is our regular kind of speech). This verse then would include praying in tongues. This verse is similar to 1 Corinthians 14:14-15.

Many times, in prayer, something just wells up on the inside of us that we cannot express in words. However, this is not something that the Holy Spirit does *apart* from us, but *in cooperation with us*. He helps us in our weaknesses of not knowing how to pray as we should. The Holy Spirit was not sent to the Earth to do anything by Himself apart from the Church. The Holy Spirit has never met anyone on the streets and saved them or healed them, but men full of the Holy Ghost do. Why didn't God just send the Holy Ghost to save that Ethiopian eunuch in the desert in Acts 8? The Holy Ghost is not sent to do the job for us but to help us do it. There are carpenters and carpenters' helpers. The carpenter is responsible for the job, not the helpers. It's the same with the Holy Ghost.

At other times, you don't feel any inspiration to pray, but sometimes, there's almost this spirit of ecstasy that overcomes you, and you feel that, if you don't pray, you're going to bust wide open. But even when there's very little inspiration, you can start out in faith and just believe that you are praying for a particular need. Smith Wigglesworth said that he'd often start out in the flesh and move into the Spirit. We don't have to wait around until we feel anointed to pray. Thank God we can move into the Spirit.

Sometimes you take hold with the Holy Spirit, and, other times, He takes hold with you first. In situations you know about or the Holy Spirit shows you, then you can initiate it and take hold with Him. But in situations you don't know about, the Holy Spirit will initiate it and begin to take hold with you as you yield to Him.

There should not be a mixture of our own will and God's will in prayer. This is why it's so important to possess a rich knowledge of the Word of God and cultivate a keen sensitivity to the Holy Spirit in prayer. That combination of the Word and the Spirit is vital to keeping prayer accurate and pure, so we can achieve the results of the fruit of answered prayer. This is an area in life and in prayer in which we should be continually growing. In the ceremonial laws of the Old Testament, we see a type and shadow of the importance of having no mixtures. Purity is important in the kingdom of God and flows over into prayer. And spiritual accuracy is vital to the fruitfulness and impact of our prayers.

"You shall keep My statutes. You shall not let your livestock breed with another kind. You shall not sow your field with mixed seed. Nor shall a garment of mixed linen and wool come upon you" (Leviticus 19:19).

I've personally witnessed a trend in many churches in recent years that has affected the purity and accuracy of our praying. There seems to be less and less prayer in the Spirit or in other tongues, and more and more prayer offered only with our own understanding that doesn't even line up with the Word of God. In other words, even the prayers offered up in our own understanding are unscriptural. This is very limited praying that will produce meager results and impact. Here is my concern as my wife and I step into our latter years.

I'm afraid that there are certain elements of prayer and intercession that will be lost to this generation unless those who are more experienced pass these things on to them by precept and example.

CHAPTER 9

PRAYER, PLANS, AND GOD'S PURPOSES

"Protect your people as they are traveling to and from church this morning."

"Bless them, Father in all they do."

"Pour out your Spirit this morning."

"We cry out for revival!"

We hear these expressions or some form of them a lot in prayer, don't we?

But we have to understand that, some things we pray for, we already have from the promises of the Word. We just need to obey the Word and/or meet the conditions. For example, some young believer could be praying for the Lord to strengthen the faith of other believers and keep them free from fear. But the Scriptures tell us that faith comes by hearing the Word of God (Romans 10:17), and we are instructed to resist the devil and the spirit of fear (James 4:7; 1 Timothy 1:7). So, faith cannot be increased and fear eliminated from the lives of believers through prayer. The Word already tells us what to do to increase faith and eliminate fear from our lives, so praying for such won't do much good.

Concerning other things, we must learn to yield and flow with God's plan and purpose for our lives and get His direction. The same would apply to our church services and times of assembling.

For example, one preacher prepared a Mother's Day sermon, but the Lord wanted to have a healing service. The man was wrestling with that thought. Well, the preacher could've prayed and prayed for God to anoint his message and the service, but God had another plan. His plan is already blessed and anointed. Our responsibility is to find and flow with His plan.

Many prayers are wasted because we are not sensitive to what the Lord wants to do or how we ought to pray, or we simply are not aligning our prayers with the Word of God. Sometimes it's not more prayer we need, but more faith and learning to yield to the Holy Spirit. If all our prayers were fruitful we'd be having revival all over the world by now. Sadly, they're not. And it's not how long our prayer chain is or how many people we can get to pray. Some 24/7 prayer movements have been nearly fruitless. Why? Because we don't know how to pray as we ought (Romans 8:26) for results. We basically ignore the One called to help us pray effectively. Some of what Christians pray for or pray about is either unscriptural, or the Word already gives us the answer. Jesus said all it takes is two or three in agreement to get the job done (Matthew 18:19). A husband and wife in agreement is enough to scatter every hindering devil in their lives.

Worship can be the same way. We sing too many songs like we are in a parade or we are conducting a concert. My old pastor used to call it 7-11 praise and worship. Sing the same 7 verses 11 times over. *Ha-ha!* The familiarity of our programmed songs and music has dulled us. When the early Church came together, they never knew what was going to happen. They were so open to the spontaneity and inspiration of the Spirit and eager to give out what they were receiving. Often, they sang their own lyrics from their own heart by the Spirit, teaching and admonishing one another in psalms, hymns, and spiritual songs. This is nearly a lost concept in the church today.

"Let the word of Christ dwell in you richly in all wisdom, teaching and admonishing one another in psalms and hymns and spiritual songs, singing with grace in your hearts to the Lord" (Colossians 3:16).

"How is it then, brethren? Whenever you come together, each of you has a psalm, has a teaching, has a tongue, has a revelation, has an interpretation. Let all things be done for edification" (1 Corinthians 14:26).

DIFFERENT PURPOSES FOR DIFFERENT MEETINGS

But not every meeting is to be like that. In Acts 20:7-12, Paul preached a long time until a young man fell asleep near the window and succumbed to his death. The Word says he died, but Paul raised him up. Apparently, Paul had much to say and much knowledge to impart to the people, and power to go with it.

Teaching is so vital to Christian growth. It's what Jesus did the most. It's what Paul and the early apostles did much of. There is a time for that. If you're having a teaching seminar, then teach. If you're having a conference, define God's purpose for that conference. You have to define the purpose of each meeting. If it's a prayer meeting, and you spend more time exhorting and talking than praying, then you've missed the purpose. If it's an evangelistic meeting to reach sinners, and you have a 1 Corinthians 14 believers meeting instead, where the focus is on believers, then you've missed it.

In Acts 8, Philip preached an evangelistic campaign. The purpose was to have healings and miracles to arrest the people's attention and save souls, and then get everyone baptized with the Holy Ghost. Not every meeting or service is the same. You have to find the theme and purpose of the Holy Ghost and channel the power.

In 1 Corinthians 14, it was mainly an assembly of believers. This is the purpose of our Holy Ghost Forums. It's a 1 Corinthians 14:26 format to teach and demonstrate the flow of the Holy Spirit by precept and example. Stick with God's purpose, and you'll see an increase in the glory and the anointing.

THINGS THAT KILL EFFECTUAL PRAYER

I'm appalled today at what passes for prayer. I've even been in fervent prayer meetings filled with passion and loud shouting, but most prayers were full of unbelief more than anything. They don't know how to channel the power. What do I mean by that? I mean people pray around the world and say everything that comes into their minds. For instance, I was in a prayer meeting recently when several different people cried out for revival using different words and phrases — mostly clichés they heard others praying, which is common today. I call it "learned behavior." But Charles Finney said that revival is no more of a miracle than a farmer preparing the ground, planting and watering the seed, and reaping a harvest. There are principles and conditions. I know this statement may be a shock to some people, but based on what Finney said, it appears that praying for revival this way seems somewhat unscriptural. Conditions must be met.

God's new covenant plan is for believers to be continually filled with the Spirit (Ephesians 5:18-19), not to cry out for revival until they're blue in the face. I know that will make the revival-chasers mad, but it's the truth. And I'm saying this as a revivalist myself and as a lifelong student of revival. But the higher way is for every believer to be continually filled with the Spirit. We need to align ourselves with the Word of God and His instructions and conditions, not our own traditions. And believe me, Pentecostals and Charismatics have many of their own traditions, especially in these aforementioned areas.

CHAPTER 10

PRAYING WITH REVELATION

It's impossible to tell of the high value derived from praying in the Spirit. The Holy Spirit helps us in all areas of life but especially in prayer. I believe the greatest advantage or benefit of being filled with the Spirit is perhaps your prayer life. Not only does it benefit you, but you can be a greater blessing and benefit to the world. The following verses speak of praying in the Spirit.

"For if I pray in a tongue, my spirit prays, but my understanding is unfruitful. What is the conclusion then? I will pray with the spirit, and I will also pray with the understanding. I will sing with the spirit, and I will also sing with the understanding" (1 Corinthians 14:14-15*).*

"Likewise the Spirit also helps in our weaknesses. For we do not know what we should pray for as we ought, but the Spirit Himself makes intercession for us with groanings which cannot be uttered" (Romans 8:26).

"...praying always with all prayer and supplication in the Spirit, *being watchful to this end with all perseverance and supplication for all the saints -* (Ephesians 6:18).

It is puzzling to me why Spirit-filled people spend so much more time praying mentally with their own understanding than *in the Spirit.* It can only be that they do not place a high value on it due to a lack of spiritual understanding and revelation.

CULTIVATING SENSITIVITY

The spiritual realm is not real to many Christians, even to those who've been Spirit-filled, because they live so much of their time in the physical and mental realm. But the most important realm is the spiritual realm. The Holy Spirit lives in our spirits and communicates with our spirits. Well, why don't we hear Him? Because we're making too much noise with our minds. That's one great advantage of praying in tongues and meditating on the Word of God. It helps keep your mind quiet. Even when you pray in tongues, your mind wants to continue making noise and thinking about this and thinking about that. The best thing you can learn to do is to set your mind upon Jesus and put it in neutral. Over time, you will become more familiar with the communion of the Holy Spirit and learn His touch.

The Holy Spirit will speak to you if you get quiet enough. He will speak to you in the nighttime or early morning, when your mind tends to be more quiet, and He will get your attention or alert you about certain things. The knowledge of those things will just come into your spirit.

He will not only speak to you about your personal life, but He will also burden you to pray for others, especially as you mature in the love of Christ. In time, as you develop your spirit, you'll be able to tell within you whether you're making intercession for a lost person, or someone who's life is in trouble or in danger, or one who is going through a test or severe trial. If someone's physical life is in danger, it will almost be like an alarm going off inside you.

FUNCTIONS OF THE HOLY SPIRIT

Remember, one of the functions of the Holy Spirit is to teach you and show you things to come, but you won't have the full manifestation of these things unless you take time to pray extensively in other tongues or in the Spirit, and your spirit has had the privilege of communing with the Father of spirits. Most of the time, it's as you pray in the Spirit that He will guide you into more truth, speak to you what He hears from Jesus and the Father, and show you things to come.

"I still have many things to say to you, but you cannot bear them now. However, when He, the Spirit of truth, has come, He will guide you into all truth; for He will not speak on His own authority, but whatever He hears He will speak; and He will tell you things to come. He will glorify Me, for He will take of what is Mine and declare it to you. All things that the Father has are Mine. Therefore I said that He will take of Mine and declare it to you" (John 16:12-15).

You see, the Holy Spirit not only helps you in making intercession, but there are also elements of teaching and revelation that He can open up to you as you learn to yield to Him and become more keen in the Spirit.

For example, in 2013, when our son went off to college, Carolyn and I began traveling and praying together more often. On a missionary trip to Colombia, the Spirit of God unveiled His plan for a new phase of ministry He wanted to launch us into, and by revelation He highlighted Ezekiel 47 to us about the rising waters that would now mark our ministry. He said, *"You have tread water long enough. It's time to launch out into the deep and swim."* We are so glad we did.

In the next few years, during our prayer times, we received more revelation than perhaps all our previous years of ministry put together. The Holy Spirit became a greater Teacher in our lives, and He not only brought many things to our remembrance, but He began to show us things to come through words of wisdom. We have more than 500 pages of prayer notes from that season of time that we journaled, and this rich communion and operation of the Holy Spirit has continued to this day. Glory to God!

Here is another part of the Spirit's ministry to us:

"His disciples did not understand these things at first; but when Jesus was glorified, then they remembered that these things were written about Him and that they had done these things to Him" (John 12:16).

Jesus is speaking of His resurrection here, which the disciples did not understand even after He repeatedly told them. Their mindset was that Jesus, as their promised Messiah, was coming to establish a physical kingdom, not to be arrested and killed. This is how it is with us many times in prayer. We have our own mindset about what we think God should do and how He should do it. That's why our mental praying is so unfruitful at times. But the Holy Spirit helps us in prayer and teaches us and gives us revelation of things to come, or what the Lord wants to do and how to pray.

In prayer, we can't always change things. At times we can only delay the inevitable, but there are spiritual and even natural laws that have been set in motion that we cannot always reverse in prayer. For example, I remember a man of prayer and of the Spirit (they often go together) being called into an intensive care unit in the hospital to pray for someone in bad shape. As soon as the man walked in, he turned around and walked back out. He knew the man would die and no amount of praying would change the situation. That man lived and prayed in the Spirit, a rarity today among so many believers and even ministers.

BRINGING THINGS TO OUR REMEMBRANCE

One of the functions of the Holy Spirit is to bring things to our remembrance as it happened after Jesus rose from the dead and was glorified. The disciples remembered what He had told them. The Holy Spirit had now come, and they began to enjoy communion with Him as they had with Jesus in the days of His Earth walk. He began to remind them of the many things that Jesus both said and did.

As I stated earlier, in our personal times of prayer, when the Holy Spirit began revealing more things to my wife and me, He would often speak to us in such terms. "Remember when ... remember this ... remember that!" One of his functions is to bring certain things to our remembrance. That is often how He teaches us. With us, He used real-life examples of years gone by and even as far back as our childhood, to teach us wisdom and lead us into all truth.

Praying in tongues or in the Spirit is the doorway into revelation knowledge and into the ministry of the Holy Spirit in teaching us and leading us into all truth and bringing things to our remembrance.

CHAPTER 11

THE HOLY SPIRIT WILL ALWAYS LEAD YOU INTO LOVE

The greatest people of prayer are people of hope, faith, and love. Hope deferred makes the heart sick, but people of prayer keep hope alive by their effectual praying.

Faith without works is dead, but people of prayer know that the greatest work of faith is to labor in prayer. Nothing of great significance happens without it.

Without love, even our speaking and praying in tongues, becomes a noisy gong and a clanging cymbal (1 Corinthians 13:1). But the true people of prayer know that love never fails.

GOD'S LOVE IS NOT SELFISH

God is not selfish. The love of God does not have a selfish bone in it. Jesus, the incarnate God, did not have one selfish cell in His body. If you want to dwell on God's frequency, then you must dwell in love.

"God is love, and he who abides in love abides in God, and God in him" (1 John 4:16b).

God does not share His wisdom with selfish saints. Your prayers are nullified in your selfishness. Selfish prayers are for babes in Christ. Maturity in love is the saintly pursuit. Wisdom lives in the bosom of those who love as Christ loved. Wisdom lives with unselfish saints.

If Christians would begin to pray for other Christians before praying for themselves, they would prosper. If churches would begin to pray for other churches before their own, they would prosper. Let us pray for other churches before praying for our own. Pray for the neighbors' children before we pray for our own. Pray for the missionaries abroad before praying for ourselves. Pray for other nations before praying for our own. True people of prayer move in this direction. That is another reason why their prayers are effectual.

Get out of selfishness. You will move into soul travail and effective intercessory prayer much faster. One church began to pray this way, and God filled it with people. Their building had a balcony that, for 15 years, never had people in it, but when they began praying this way, it filled up. You possess a city through this kind of love which will move you into soul travail and deeper intercessory prayer.

Praying only with your own understanding is selfish praying. Praying in the Spirit or in other tongues is unselfish.

CHAPTER 12

NEW REALMS

When are you going to get going and touch new realms for God? Well, do you believe you can do that without being filled and refilled with the Holy Spirit and speaking in tongues *"more than you all"* (1 Corinthians 14:18)?

It will never happen. When the late Kenneth E. Hagin began to touch new realms in God, he testified that he received more revelation in six months' time than the previous fourteen years he had in early ministry. Tongues gives birth to revelation and is a stream that should never run dry.

How do you think the apostle Paul received revelation to be able to pen more than half of the New Testament?

The Spirit realm is more real than the natural realm. The third heaven was so staggering for the apostle Paul that he couldn't even talk about it.

"...I will go on to visions and revelations of the Lord. I know a man in Christ who fourteen years ago—whether in the body or out of the body I do not know, God knows—was caught up to the third heaven. And I know that this man—whether in the body or away from the body I do not know, God knows—was caught up into paradise, and he heard utterances beyond the power of man to put into words, which man is not permitted to utter" (2 Corinthians 12:1b-4 — AMPC).

Phil Halverson was a mighty intercessor who prayed in the realm of the Spirit. What a gentle soul he was, but, in the Spirit, he was a lion. When he came to my Bible school to share, heaven fell when he began to pray. Hundreds of students fell to their faces and began to pray as we were overcome by the spirit of prayer. That experience was worth one thousand sermons to me. This man knew God, and yet, he was a simple layman, not a ministry gift.

Do you know how this dear man died? In prayer. He was called to the platform in a church service and fell prostrate in deep prayer. In a short time, he was gone.

His spirit got out too far in that other realm, and he never came back. Kind of like an astronaut in outer space whose tether snaps. He then floats into oblivion and is lost forever. The Spirit realm is the same way.

Oh, dear friends — that's our home. As citizens of heaven, that's our realm. We should become more familiar with it down here. You can cultivate the ability to move in that realm through being saturated in the Word and soaked in the fresh oil of the Holy Spirit. Tongues is where you start.

China missionary Jackie Pullinger, was a non-believer in tongues until some other missionaries taught her the value and importance of it. It took a little time to convince her using the Scriptures. But soon she was baptized with the Holy Spirit and set her heart to pray in tongues each day for at least 30 minutes. She began praying for the drug addicts she had been unsuccessfully ministering to for some time and now seeing them delivered. Doctors were astonished and she told them her secret — she had power now from praying in tongues. Her ministry was revolutionized and many sent the street people and drug addicts to her to be delivered, housed, and discipled. Jackie is now known all over the world for her work in China's Hong Kong region. Friends, this is reality! It is the reason and purpose of why Jesus sent the early disciples to Jerusalem's upper room to wait for that power from on high that was initially evidenced by speaking in tongues.

Why do you think the devil has worked overtime to make this prayer language so confusing and controversial? In the past decade, as the true Church was rising, he so insidiously infiltrated many of our churches with man's wisdom until we lost the ability to move in the power of God. He removed tongues from many of our so-called full gospel churches, leaving a void that the devil began to fill with heathenism.

Slowly the preaching of sin, repentance, and hell eroded, and the most popular preachers in America became trophies of Satan. He proudly paraded them in that invisible realm before principalities and powers, and soon we were having visible parades on this Earth realm of Sodom and Gomorrah marches. The churches are to blame for that abomination.

That empty void was filled by heathenism. It's been that way throughout the centuries. Any church that is void of the moving of the Spirit of God, beginning with the removal of "*tongues,*" will soon lose its life-giving power and start dying. From then on, it's a downward cycle. Some will eventually become synagogues of Satan. Oh, dear friends, the devil is playing for keeps.

A barren church is a breeding ground for doctrines of demons. Our churches should be a breeding ground for miracles and the power and presence of God.

The Lord spoke to me at the beginning of the so-called seeker-friendly movement when "attraction" churches were rising up everywhere. In order to boost attendance and make visitors feel welcome, unwise pastors toned down on speaking and singing in tongues. Any manifestations of the Holy Spirit became rare. "It will scare the visitor; it will offend the seeker," they said. The Lord led me and my wife to move in the opposite direction very quickly and with strength.

As churches began to build on the philosophies of men and human wisdom prevailed, soon there was a diabolical silence on holiness. Of course! The devil hates anything that is holy. The Holy Spirit is the Spirit of holiness by which Christ lived and was resurrected.

The Lord Jesus Christ was "*declared to be the Son of God with power according to the Spirit of holiness, by the resurrection from the dead*" (Romans 1:4).

A FINAL WARNING

Don't make peace with impotence. Don't accept any lesser standard than what Jesus established and set. Don't settle for powerlessness.

Listen friends, there has been a definite measured decline in the power of God in many of our churches today. I believe this decline is directly connected to the lack of emphasis on the baptism with the Holy Spirit, and tongues specifically, and over recent decades this is also directly linked to the rise of Woke-ism and the Marxist mania filling the void that's been left by the retreating church.

It is not a time to retreat but to advance. The saltiest Christians are those baptized with the Holy Spirit. Their power is the resistance the devil fears. They are the restrainers of evil in this world and their effectual prayers in the Spirit execute Satan's defeat in this age.

Let's welcome the Holy Spirit back into our churches. Let's end the diabolical silence on holiness. Let's surround the sacred baptism with the Holy Spirit and tongues with the reverence it deserves.

That's what love would do.

CHAPTER 13

HOW TO MINISTER THE HOLY SPIRIT TO OTHERS

Every Spirit-baptized believer should be equipped to minister the baptism with the Holy Spirit to others. What I'm sharing in this chapter are truths and principles I've used for over 40 years, with pretty good success, to help candidates receive the Holy Spirit with the initial evidence of speaking in other tongues. My hope is that these truths will help and equip you to minister the same to others.

In larger campaigns and some denominational churches I've ministered in, and even one-on-one, I have often ministered salvation and the Holy Spirit baptism in the same setting. In other words, I lead people to Jesus and then minister the baptism with the Holy Spirit to them. So, the first thing I make sure of is that candidates have come to sincere repentance, and that there is no known unforgiveness in their heart, especially in older believers who've never been baptized with the Holy Spirit. I have found unforgiveness to be one of the greatest hindrances for Christians receiving anything from God.

"Then Peter said to them, "__Repent,__ and let every one of you be baptized in the name of Jesus Christ for the remission of sins; and you shall __receive__ the __gift__ of the Holy Spirit" (Acts 2:38).

Notice the three words I've highlighted in the above scripture. Unless the Spirit of God leads me differently, this is where I focus most of my attention in ministering the Holy Spirit baptism to people.

1. Repentance
2. Receive
3. Gift

Repentance from dead works and faith toward God are the first principles of the doctrine of Christ (Hebrews 6). Once candidates repent, they need to exercise their faith toward God. Everything we receive from God comes by grace through faith.

There are many man-made traditions, even in Full Gospel theology today, that hinder people from receiving. For example, people often think they have to do certain things, or somehow clean up their lives, before they can receive the fullness of the Holy Spirit. Those beliefs are a part of dead works. If the person has genuinely come to repentance and has been cleansed by the blood of Jesus, there is nothing the candidate can do to improve on that. The blood of Jesus is enough, and it is what qualifies people to receive the Holy Spirit. When they are born again their spirit is recreated and their nature changes. Their sin nature is removed (that's what the word *"remission"* means in the aforementioned Acts 2:38) and they become a new creation in Christ. This alone qualifies any believer to receive the Holy Spirit with the initial evidence of speaking in other tongues.

THE HOLY SPIRIT IS A GIFT TO BE RECEIVED

Furthermore, the Holy Spirit is a gift. Believers cannot earn the Holy Spirit by what they do or don't do, or any sacrifices they make. If they could, then He ceases to be a gift.

"If a son asks for bread from any father among you, will he give him a stone? Or if he asks for a fish, will he give him a serpent instead of a fish? Or if he asks for an egg, will he offer him a scorpion? If you then, being evil, know how to give good gifts to your children, how much more will your heavenly Father give the Holy Spirit to those who ask Him" (Luke 11:11-13)!

Not only must you let the candidate know that the Holy Spirit is a gift, but you must also let him know that he will not receive any counterfeit or strange spirit; the Heavenly Father will give him exactly what he asks for. In fact, in God's mind, the Holy Spirit has already been given. Our responsibility is to receive. The early apostles prayed for candidates to receive the *gift* of the Holy Spirit, not necessarily for God to give it.

"Now when the apostles who were at Jerusalem heard that Samaria had received the word of God, they sent Peter and John to them, who, when they had come down, prayed for them that they might receive the Holy Spirit" (Acts 8:14-15).

TONGUES COMES WITH THE HOLY SPIRIT

I have made it a practice over the years to help candidates cooperate with God in receiving not only the Holy Spirit but their prayer language as well. Unless you have a special grace or endowment in laying hands on believers to receive the Holy Spirit, as Peter and John did, you should give them sufficient instruction to help them understand, cooperate, and receive the Holy Spirit and their prayer language. Most of the time, this instruction is the difference between success and failure in ministering the baptism with the Holy Spirit to people. Faith and expectation will increase in candidates when they hear sound instruction from the word of God.

In classes, meetings, or one-on-one ministry I've conducted over the years, I'd get people so excited about receiving the Holy Spirit that they'd begin receiving and speaking in tongues before I even prayed for them because their expectation was so great. You can learn to do that too, if you're not already doing it. Faith and expectation comes by hearing the word of God (Romans 10:17).

You don't have to be an Ephesians 4:11 ministry gift or a great teacher to minister the Holy Spirit to people. Any Spirit-filled saint can pray and lay hands on another believer by faith to receive the Holy Spirit — with the initial evidence of speaking in tongues. I'm a firm believer that every born again, Spirit-filled Christian should thoroughly know and be confident in ministering salvation, the Holy Spirit, and healing to anyone. This is the believer's commission.

As I've already stated, the greatest hindrance to receiving the Holy Spirit is usually unforgiveness. If there's a devil in the way, the Lord will let you know that too. However, it has been my personal experience over the years that another great hurdle or obstacle in people receiving the Holy Spirit along with their prayer language (tongues) is a misunderstanding or misconception that many have about receiving. **Many think it's the Holy Spirit who does the speaking, and not really them.** Sometimes I have to spend a considerable amount of time on this point before I feel a release to minister to them.

For example, recently I ministered to a young believer, and I could actually see the Spirit of God on him. He was shaking and crying but never spoke in tongues. Afterwards, I spent a little more time with him because the Lord showed me what his problem was. I asked him if he sensed the presence of God when

I prayed for him. He said he did. Then I asked him if there was something bubbling up inside of him and moving on his vocal chords. He replied again that there was. I told him that this was the Holy Spirit giving him utterance to speak. Then I asked him why he didn't yield to this utterance, or prompting, to speak. He then told me that he was scared. After I dealt with his fear, I then got him to yield to the Holy Spirit again, and he spoke in tongues fluently. Praise the Lord! He didn't realize that the Holy Spirit was actually trying to help him receive his prayer language and granting him utterance to speak in tongues.

TEACHING THE CANDIDATE TO COOPERATE WITH THE HOLY SPIRIT

Acts 2:4 is one of the scriptures I often use to show candidates the cooperation that is necessary to receive the Holy Spirit.

*"And **they** were all filled with the Holy Spirit and **(they)** began to speak with other tongues, **as the Spirit** gave them utterance."*

Who spoke in tongues? The people did.

Who gave them the utterance or enabled them to speak in tongues? The Holy Spirit did.

This scripture is usually where I spend the most time.

Sometimes, the lack of understanding of this simple concept elicits some pretty humorous responses from candidates trying to receive their prayer language.

I've had tight-lipped candidates refuse to move their mouths for fear they'd get in the flesh. I've had others just open their mouth and expect God to fill it — like they just swallowed a radio and were expecting it to play when they opened their mouths. Unless there is a real anointing and manifestation of the Spirit, it is always reasonable and more productive to instruct him how to receive the Holy Spirit and speak in other tongues for the first time. People need faith and understanding to receive. You have to tell them what to expect.

"If anyone thirsts, <u>let him come to Me and drink</u>. He who believes in Me, as the Scripture has said, 'out of his belly will flow rivers of living water.' But this He

spoke concerning the Spirit, whom those believing in Him would receive" (John 7:37b-39a).

Jesus said to come and drink. You can't drink with your mouth closed. Instruct the candidate not to speak a single word in his native language. You cannot speak two languages at once. At times, I may even tell the candidate that he is grieving the Holy Spirit by speaking in a known language. It takes faith to yield to an unknown tongue.

Again, instruct the candidate that speaking in tongues is an act of cooperation between him and the Holy Spirit. It's not all the Holy Spirit and it's not all him. Tell him that the Holy Spirit will give him utterance and that his tongue will want to say something. I have found this to be true in nearly every case.

It is helpful to encourage the candidate to relax and fearlessly and boldly lift up his voice and yield to the utterance and supernatural sounds that are waiting to find expression through his own tongue and lips.

When you see the Holy Spirit moving on the candidate's lips and tongue, encourage him to speak any sounds or words that seem easiest to speak, regardless of what they sound like. Then tell him to continue to speak supernatural words in praise to God until a clear free-flowing language comes forth and you and him have an assurance, and there's a witness in him, that he has received.

There's an inspiration that comes on the candidate to speak in other tongues. *"Inspiration"* means to breathe in the Spirit of God. In ministering the Holy Spirit to people, at times I'll have them look to the Lord and just take a deep breath by inhaling or drinking of the Spirit of God. This also helps them relax and be filled with the Holy Spirit by faith. Some people hear supernatural words inside their inner being, and the words bubble up until they release them out of their mouth.

In others, there might be a fluttering or a stammering of the lips. The Holy Spirit does this because the lips and the tongue are the members of the physical body that form words. This is how the Holy Spirit gives utterance to people and prompts them to speak. But ultimately, it is the believer that must do the speaking.

Finally, if you are in a group setting, it is best to take the candidate aside to instruct him in the baptism with the Holy Spirit in a one-on-one setting. If many people crowd around the candidate, conflicting instructions might get offered, which could make him uncomfortable and only produce fear and anxiety. It is more difficult for the candidate to receive when he is not comfortable and relaxed. I was personally ministered to in this manner, in a small group setting, and in spite of the group's ignorance, I did receive a light anointing of the Holy Spirit and spoke a few syllables in tongues. But I also felt like I was cheated out of a greater utterance and blessing that I could've received. Instead, I had to wait another two or three weeks to enter into the fullness of the Spirit's blessing and a freer-flowing prayer language of new tongues.

Since this book is entitled, *Tongues: The Elevation Of A Mystery,* I have shared these lengthy and thorough instructions on how to actually lead the candidate in releasing his prayer language. Often, that's where the challenge is. Some might be wondering, *"Can't people receive the power of the Holy Spirit without speaking in tongues?"* I do not believe the Scriptures teach that, and there are really no examples of it in the Word, so you cannot build a doctrine or practice on that. Speaking in tongues comes with the power of the Holy Spirit, and if candidates don't speak in tongues, I believe it is a waste.

I hope these instructions are a blessing to you and will help you be bold and confident in ministering the Holy Spirit to others.

CHAPTER 14

NEW TESTAMENT PRAYERS

"Then He said to His disciples, 'The harvest truly is plentiful, but the laborers are few. Therefore pray the Lord of the harvest to send out laborers into His harvest'" (Matthew 9:37-38).

"I do not pray for these alone, but also for those who will believe in Me through their word; that they all may be one, as You, Father, are in Me, and I in You; that they also may be one in Us, that the world may believe that You sent Me. And the glory which You gave Me I have given them, that they may be one just as We are one: I in them, and You in Me; that they may be made perfect in one, and that the world may know that You have sent Me, and have loved them as You have loved Me" (John 17:20-23).

"Now, Lord, look on their threats, and grant to Your servants that with all boldness they may speak Your word, by stretching out Your hand to heal, and that signs and wonders may be done through the name of Your holy Servant Jesus" (Acts 4:29-31).

"Now I beg you, brethren, through the Lord Jesus Christ, and through the love of the Spirit, that you strive together with me in prayers to God for me, that I may be delivered from those in Judea who do not believe, and that my service for Jerusalem may be acceptable to the saints, that I may come to you with joy by the will of God, and may be refreshed together with you. Now the God of peace be with you all. Amen" (Romans 15:30-33).

"Therefore I also, after I heard of your faith in the Lord Jesus and your love for all the saints, do not cease to give thanks for you, making mention of you in my prayers: that the God of our Lord Jesus Christ, the Father of glory, may give to you the spirit of wisdom and revelation in the knowledge of Him, the eyes of your understanding being enlightened; that you may know what is the hope of His calling, what are the riches of the glory of His inheritance in the saints, and what is the exceeding greatness of His power toward us who believe, according to the working of His mighty power

which He worked in Christ when He raised Him from the dead and seated Him at His right hand in the heavenly places, far above all principality and power and might and dominion, and every name that is named, not only in this age but also in that which is to come. And He put all things under His feet, and gave Him to be head over all things to the church, which is His body, the fullness of Him who fills all in all" (Ephesians 1:15-23).

"*For this reason I bow my knees to the Father of our Lord Jesus Christ, from whom the whole family in heaven and earth is named, that He would grant you, according to the riches of His glory, to be strengthened with might through His Spirit in the inner man, that Christ may dwell in your hearts through faith; that you, being rooted and grounded in love, may be able to comprehend with all the saints what is the width and length and depth and height — to know the love of Christ which passes knowledge; that you may be filled with all the fullness of God. Now to Him who is able to do exceedingly abundantly above all that we ask or think, according to the power that works in us, to Him be glory in the church by Christ Jesus to all generations, forever and ever. Amen*" (Ephesians 3:14-21).

"*...praying always with all prayer and supplication in the Spirit, being watchful to this end with all perseverance and supplication for all the saints — and for me, that utterance may be given to me, that I may open my mouth boldly to make known the mystery of the gospel*" (Ephesians 6:18-19).

"*And this I pray, that your love may abound still more and more in knowledge and all discernment, that you may approve the things that are excellent, that you may be sincere and without offense till the day of Christ, being filled with the fruits of righteousness which are by Jesus Christ, to the glory and praise of God*" (Philippians 2:9-11).

"*For this reason we also, since the day we heard it, do not cease to pray for you, and to ask that you may be filled with the knowledge of His will in all wisdom and spiritual understanding; that you may walk worthy of the Lord, fully pleasing Him, being fruitful in every good work and increasing in the knowledge of God; strengthened with all might, according to His glorious power, for all patience and longsuffering with joy*" (Colossians 1:9-11).

"Continue earnestly in prayer, being vigilant in it with thanksgiving; meanwhile praying also for us, that God would open to us a door for the word, to speak the mystery of Christ, for which I am also in chains, that I may make it manifest, as I ought to speak" (Colossians 4:2-4).

"Now may our God and Father Himself, and our Lord Jesus Christ, direct our way to you. And may the Lord make you increase and abound in love to one another and to all, just as we do to you, so that He may establish your hearts blameless in holiness before our God and Father at the coming of our Lord Jesus Christ with all His saints" (1 Thessalonians 3:11-13).

"Therefore we also pray always for you that our God would count you worthy of this calling, and fulfill all the good pleasure of His goodness and the work of faith with power, that the name of our Lord Jesus Christ may be glorified in you, and you in Him, according to the grace of our God and the Lord Jesus Christ" (2 Thessalonians 1:11-12).

"Finally, brethren, pray for us, that the word of the Lord may run swiftly and be glorified, just as it is with you, and that we may be delivered from unreasonable and wicked men; for not all have faith" (2 Thessalonians 3:1-2).

"Therefore I exhort first of all that supplications, prayers, intercessions, and giving of thanks be made for all men, for kings and all who are in authority, that we may lead a quiet and peaceable life in all godliness and reverence. For this is good and acceptable in the sight of God our Savior, who desires all men to be saved and to come to the knowledge of the truth" (1 Timothy 2:1-4).

ABOUT THE AUTHOR

Bert M. Farias, together with his wife, Carolyn, graduates of Rhema Bible Training Center, served as missionaries in West Africa for many years before founding Holy Fire Ministries in 1997, a ministry committed to carrying the spirit of prayer and revival to the Church and the nations.

Bert and Carolyn have now entered the final phase of their life and ministry with a mandate to father and mentor the younger generations, according to Psalms 71:17-18:

O God, You have taught me from my youth; and to this day I declare Your wondrous works. Now also when I am old and gray-headed, O God, do not forsake me, until I declare Your strength to this generation, Your power to everyone who is to come.

Before being separated solely to the full-time preaching and teaching ministry, Bert experienced a unique and powerful baptism of fire. His consuming passion is for human beings to come into a real and vibrant relationship with the Lord Jesus Christ through the power of the Holy Spirit and to become passionate workers in His kingdom.

With a divine commission to also write, Bert has authored multiple books with an emphasis on helping to restore the true spirit of Christianity in the Church today and preparing the saints for the glory of God, the harvest, and the imminent return of the Lord.

- "Right now, your calling is evangelistic in function but apostolic in nature. But, in your later years, it will be reversed to be apostolic in function but still evangelistic in nature." (circa 1989)

- "For some have said to you: What is your vision? For you have no building or systematic organization of any kind, but your vision is to build a city not made with hands — to take a people to a place where I am, sojourners in a land, a vision not of man. Yours is a vision in the Spirit to redeem man; a vision to furnish the inside of man, for they are the true temple of God. My plan for which you've been created is to build man. Draw forth in prayer the provision of My wisdom for My people."

- "Writing is your life's greatest work."

MINISTRY INFORMATION

To become a monthly partner with Holy Fire Ministries, to schedule a speaking engagement with Bert and/or Carolyn, to receive a free monthly newsletter, or to follow Bert's blog, please visit our website: **www.holy-fire.org**[1]

HOLY FIRE MINISTRIES

PO Box 4527

Windham, NH 03087

Email: holyfiremin@comcast.net

---

1. http://www.holy-fire.org